CLOUDY, WITH A CHANGE OF TOASTED RAV

Written and illustrated by Ryan Nusbickel

MAUREEN- DON'T FORGET THE MARINARA!

For the St. Louis foodie, in each of us.

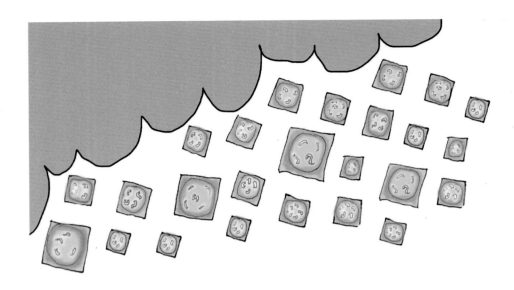

"In the Spring, I have counted 136 different kinds of weather inside of 24 hours."
- Mark Twain

"It's not the heat. It's the humidity."
- St. Louis Proverb

It's a St. Louis saying that always rings true:
Don't like the weather? Wait a minute or two!

You name it. We get it. From mist to monsoon,
with fog, wind, snow and sunshine all before noon.

But no St. Louis weather will ever compare
to that curious storm that began raining giant, golden squares.

7

It was raining toasted ravioli! It really was!
Titantic t-ravs sprinkling down from above.

Each ravioli, so crispy and covered with parm,
landing everywhere from Old St. Charles ...

9

To Grant's Farm.

MoDOT crews plowed and put down salt to prevent slipping.

They switched to marinara sauce which made for better dipping.

And toasted ravioli wasn't all that fell from the skies.
Next came pork steaks, Red Hot Riplets, and thin crust pizza pies.

And huge plates of slingers sizzled as they glided down,

With chili that covered baseball fans from out of town.

Then came a drenching of ranch dressing, like a storm in Spring.

Ranch on the Arch. Ranch on the zoo.

Ranch dressing on everything.

TV weather crews were shocked by the precipitation that day.
Their TV weather maps looked like a St. Louis buffet.

And ballpark snacks fell on Busch Stadium. Fans cheered like it was a grand slam.

And the biggest plate of nachos in history even made it on the "Kiss Cam."

Around the World's Fair Pavilion, The Art Museum, and the Muny ...

Fell ice cream cones, iced tea, and tons of cotton candy.

Another blast from the past arrived: French onion soup from Famous Barr.

24

Each wave of weather moved in along Interstate 70 and Farty-Farr.

And on South Grand Avenue, falafel fell like snow …

Along with lepinja bread, tajine, pad thai, and pho.

A lotta muffalettas fell in Benton Park, along with pretzels eaten with mustard.

And on Steinberg rink, kids ice skated on gobs of frozen custard.

Scotch oatmeal cookies became float trip rafts. They were a sweet ride.

And the biggest BLTs you ever saw fell on the city's North Side.

St. Paul sammies caused river jammies, for more than twenty miles,

While kids skateboarded on barbecue ribs, cut St. Louis style.

On the Hill a gale of antipasto began to blow,

With mortadella, mozzarella, and pepperoncini. *Bellisimo!*

St. Louis city and county even threw out the divorce.

They celebrated on gooey butter cake. I HAD to mention THAT treat of course!

From a tsunami of hot salami, to a white haze of Soulard beignets.

To a landslide of Friday fish fries, we saw the whole St. Louis menu that day.

While this storm kept all ages of St. Louis well-fed,

40

Some couldn't help running to grocery stores for their milk, eggs, and bread.

Until finally, the storm left, as quickly as it had come.

A spread of food was left in its wake, but it was gobbled up. Every crumb!

And soon it became St. Louis legend: The Toasted Rav Tempest of long ago.

More of a blessing than a curse. It could have been worse.
At least we weren't Chicago.

ST. LOUIS TRIVIA TAKE-OUT

1. In addition to ice cream cones, cotton candy, and iced tea, what else was introduced at the 1904 World's Fair in St. Louis?

A. The hot dog
B. The "Power Play Dance"
C. Halloween jokes

2. What is inside a St. Paul Sandwich?

A. Leftover slinger chili
B. Egg Foo Young
C. Salcissia brined in the tears of baseball fans from the Chicago Northside

3. Red Hot Riplets are often incorporated in which of the following St Louis dishes?

A. Sprinkled over a provel pizza
B. Layered inside a hot chicken sandwich
C. Dumped on a saucy pork steak
D. All of the above

4. Pork steak comes from what cut of the pig?

A. The butt
B The snoot
C. Who cares. It's fall off the bone tender and it's PORK.
D. A. and C.

5. Provel cheese is a delicious blend of what three cheeses?

A. Mozzarella, provclone, and cheddar
B. Cheddar, provclone, and swiss
C. Provclone, cotswold, and manchego

1.A.   2.B.   3.D.   4.D.   5.B.

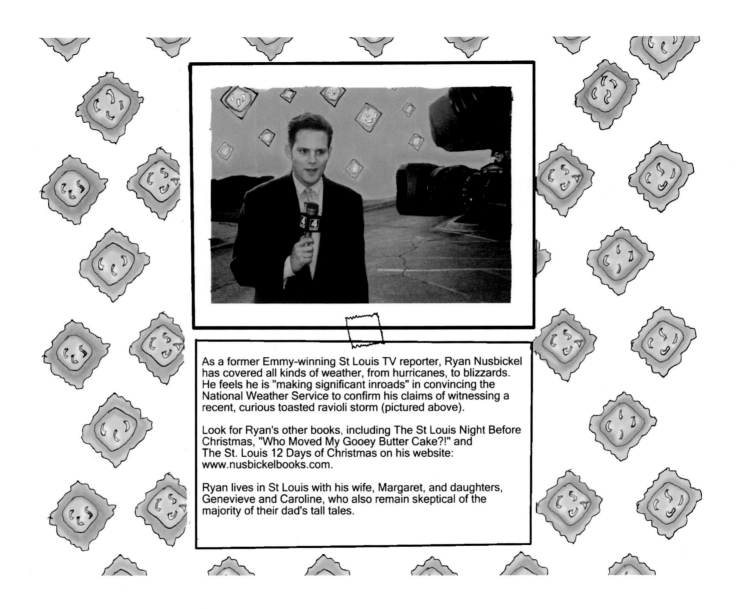

As a former Emmy-winning St Louis TV reporter, Ryan Nusbickel has covered all kinds of weather, from hurricanes, to blizzards. He feels he is "making significant inroads" in convincing the National Weather Service to confirm his claims of witnessing a recent, curious toasted ravioli storm (pictured above).

Look for Ryan's other books, including The St Louis Night Before Christmas, "Who Moved My Gooey Butter Cake?!" and The St. Louis 12 Days of Christmas on his website: www.nusbickelbooks.com.

Ryan lives in St Louis with his wife, Margaret, and daughters, Genevieve and Caroline, who also remain skeptical of the majority of their dad's tall tales.

Also by Ryan Nusbickel ...

It's the Night Before Christmas story
(with gooey butter cake.)

Because Christmas in St. Louis is
too much fun for just one day!

"The book for the St. Louisan who has
everything."
-FEAST MAGAZINE

All of Ryan's books can be
purchased on his website:
www.nusbickelbooks.com.

Made in the USA
Middletown, DE
29 October 2017